100

No Man
Is an Island

No Man Is an Island

Selected from the writings of John Donne

Edited by Keith Fallon

STANYAN BOOKS   RANDOM HOUSE

A Stanyan book published by Stanyan Books,
8721 Sunset Blvd., Los Angeles, California,
and, by Random House, Inc.,
201 E. 50th St., New York, N.Y.

Printed in the United States of America

Design / Anthony Goldschmidt

To Joyce and Sparky Schulz

No man is an island, entire of itself;
every man is a piece of the continent,
a part of the main; if a clod be
washed away by the sea, Europe is the less,
as well as if a promontory were, as well
as if a manor of thy friends or of thine
own were; any man's death diminishes me,
because I am involved in mankind; and
therefore never send to know for whom the
bell tolls; it tolls for thee.

I am of opinion, that nothing is so potent
either to procure, or merit Love, as Valour,
and I am glad I am so, for thereby
I shall do my self much ease. Because valour
never needs much wit to maintain it.

I am two fools,
I know,
For loving,
and for saying so.

Teach me to hear Mermaides singing

Send home
my long strayed eyes to me,
which, oh, too long
have dwelt on thee.

Oh do not die
For I shall hate
All women so,
When thou art gone

Even at your noon and warmest Sunshine
of prosperity, you owe yourselves a true
information, how you came by that
prosperity, who gave it to you, and why he
gave it. Let not the Olive boast of her own
fatness, nor the Figtree of her own sweetness,
nor the Vine of her own fruitfulness, for
we were all but Brambles. Let no man say,
I could not miss a fortune, for I have studied
all my youth; How many men have studied
more nights, than he hath done hours, and
studied themselves blind, and mad in the
Mathematiques, and yet withers in beggery
in a corner?

A scar in a man's face
is the same as a mole
in a woman's, and a
mole in a woman's
is a jewel set in white
to make it seem more white.

He that brags of his own
dissuades others from believing it.

My face is thine eye,
thine is mine.

I would not make man
more worse than he is,
nor his condition
more miserable than it is.

A man may live
of a little;
but, alas, of how much less
may a man die.

Now thou hast lov'd me one whole day,
Tomorrow when thou leav'st,
what wilt thou say?

God hath not made a week without a Sabbath; no tentation, without an issue; God inflicts no calamity, no cloud, no eclipse, without light, to see ease in it, if the patient will look upon that which God hath done to him, in other cases, or to that which God hath done to others, at other times. Saul fell to the ground, but he fell no lower; God brings us to humiliation, but not to desperation.

Blasted with sighs,
and surrounded with teares,
Hither I come to seeke the spring.

If yet I have not all they love,
Deare, I shall never have it all.

My best days
are when I shake with fear.

I long to talk
with some old lover's ghost
who died before
the god of love
was born.

Men are to have their turns, to take their time, and then to give way by death to successors; and so it is Incivile, inofficiosum, not to be content to die, it opposes the frame and form of government. It comes equally to us all, and makes us all equal when it comes. The ashes of an Oak in the Chimney, are no Epitaph of that Oak, to tell me how high or how large that was; It tells me not what flocks it sheltered while it stood, nor what men it hurt when it fell. The dust of great persons' graves is speechless too, it says nothing.

Age is a sickness and Youth is an ambush;
and we need so many Physicians,
as may make up a Watch, and spy every
inconvenience.

As all shadows are of one color, if you respect the body from which they are cast, (for our shadows upon clay will be dirty, and in a garden green and flowery) so all retirings into a shadowy life are alike from all causes, and alike subject to the barbarousness and insipid dullness of the Country: only the employments, and that upon which you cast and bestow your pleasure, business, or books, gives it the tincture, and beauty. But truly wheresoever we are, if we can but tell ourselves truly what and where we would be, we may make any state and place such.

What is so intricate
so entangling
as death?

My Body licenseth my soul to see the world's beauties through mine eyes: to hear pleasant things through mine ears; and affords it apt Organs for the convenience of all perceivable delight.

Friendship has so much of Soveraignty,
yes and of Religion too, that no prescription
can be admitted against it. And as for losing
you by any forfeit, or demerit on my part,

I have been very careful, and shall be watchful still, to bless myself from such a curse, as that. And indeed, such care is all the merit, which can be hoped for, at the hands of a person, so useless as myself. And from this care now proceeds my haste, to thank you for your last Letter; and to beg a preservation of that love, which though, at first, it fell not directly, and immediately upon myself, but by way of reflection or Briccole, through your other Friends (to use the Metaphor of a Game, wherein I congratulate that excellency, to which my Lord Clifford tells me, you have arrived) yet now I dare conceive, that your love belongs to me, even as a kind of due, since I see, you now discern that I am so much in earnest in loving you.

He is starke mad, who ever sayes,
That he hath been in love an houre.

A man truly liberal, or truly charitable,
will borrow money to lend.

The Spanish proverb informs me, that
he is a fool which cannot make one Sonnet,
and he is mad which makes two.

We die every day, and we die all the day long;
and because we are not absolutely dead,
we call that an eternity, an eternity of dying;
And is there comfort in that state? why,
that is the state of hell itself, Eternal Dying,
and not dead.

Men and women call one another inconstant,
and accuse one another of having changed
their minds, when God knows, they have but
changed the object of their eye, and seen
a better white or red. An old man loves not
the same sports that he did when he was
young, nor a sick man the same meats that
he did when he was well: But these men
have not changed their minds; The old man
has changed his fancy, and the sick man
his taste; neither his mind.

To stand inquiring right,
is not to stray;
to sleep, or run wrong, is.

Sleep is pains easiest salve
and fulfills all offices of death,
except to kill.

I observe the Physician, with the same
diligence, as he the disease; I see he fears

and I fear with him: I overtake him, I overrun him in his fear, and I go the faster, because he makes his pace slow; I fear the more, because he disguises his fear, and I see it with the more sharpness, because he would not have me see it. He knows that his fear shall not disorder the practice, and exercise of his Art, but he knows that my fear may disorder the effect, and working of his practice. As the ill affections of the spleen, complicate, and mingle themselves with every infirmity of the body, so does fear insinuate itself in every action or passion of the mind; and as the wind in the body will counterfeit any disease, and seem the stone and seem the Gout, so fear will counterfeit any disease of the Mind; It shall seem love, a love of having, and it is but a fear, a jealous, and suspicious fear of loosing.

They have hotter days in Spain than
we have here, but our days are longer; and
yet we are hotter in our business here,
and they longer about it there. God is
sometimes called a Giant, running a race; and
sometimes is so slowpaced, as that a
thousand years make but a day with Him.

The difference between the Reason of man, and the Instinct of the beast is this, That the beast does but know, but the man knows what he knows.

All eggs are not hatched
that the hen sits upon.

The Flea, though he kill none,
he does all the harm he can.

More than kisses,
letters mingle souls;
For, thus friends absent speak.

For god's sake
hold your tongue,
and let me love.

I die as often
as from thee I go.

Evill Manners are Parents of good Lawes;
and in every Evill there is an excellency,
which (in common speech) we call good.
For the fashions of habits, for our moving in
gestures; for phrases in our speech, we say
they are good as long as they were used,
that is, as long as they were common; and
we eat, we walk, only when it is, or seems
good to do so.

Valor towards men
is an emblem
of an ability
toward women.

THE GOOD TOMORROW

I wonder by my troth, what thou, and I
Did, till we lov'd?
   were we not wean'd till then?
But suck'd on countrey pleasures, childishly?
Or snorted we in the seaven sleepers den?
T'was so; But this, all pleasures fancies bee.
If ever any beauty I did see,
Which I desir'd, and got,
   t'was but a dreame of thee.

And now good morrow to our waking soules,
Which watch not one another out of feare;
For love, all love of other sights controules,
And makes one little roome, an every where.
Let sea-discoverers to new worlds have gone,
Let Maps to other, worlds on worlds
    have showne,
Let us possesse one world, each hath one,
    and is one.

My face in thine eye, thine in mine appeares,
And true plaine hearts doe in the faces rest,
Where can we find two better hemispheares
Without sharpe North,
    without declining West?
What ever dyes, was not mixt equally;
If our two loves be one, or, thou and I
Love so alike, that none doe slacken,
    none can die.

Full nakedness!
All joys are due to thee,
as souls unbodied,
bodies unclothed must be,
to taste whole joys.

I have a great desire, not without some hope, to see you this Summer there; and I have more hope and more desire, to see you this next Winter here; and I have abundantly more of both, that, at least, we shall meet in Heaven. That we differ in our ways, I hope we pardon one another. Men go to China, both by the Straights, and by the Cape.

When God came to breath into Man
the breath of life, he found him flat upon
the ground; when he comes to withdraw that
breath from him again, he prepares him to it,
by laying him flat upon his bed.

It is an excuse to them that are great, and pretend, and yet are lothe to come; it is an inhibition to those who would truly come, because they may be made instruments, and pestiducts, to the infection of others, by their comming.

I am no great voyager in other men's works: no swallower nor devourer of volumes nor pursuant of authors. Perchance it is because

I find borne in my self knowledge or apprehension enough, for (without forfeiture or impeachment of modesty) I think I am bond to God thankfully to acknowledge it, to consider him and myself: as when I have at home a convenient garden I covet not to walk in others broad meadows or woods, especially because it falls not within that short reach which my foresight embraceth, to see how I should employ that which I already know; to travail for inquiry of more were to labor to get a stomach and then find no meat at home. To know how to live by the book is a pedantry, and to do it is bondage.

I have noted some, which not understanding
jests, etc., have yet chosen this as the
best means to seem wise and understanding,
to laugh when their Companions laugh;
and I have presumed them ignorant, whom
I have seen unmoved. A fool if he come
into a Princes Court, and see a gay man
leaning at the wall, so glistering, and so
painted in many colours that he is hardly
discerned from one of the Pictures in the
Arras hanging, his body like an Ironbound
chest, girt in and thick ribb'd with broad
gold laces, may (and commonly doth)
envy him.

But alas! shall a <u>wise man</u>, which may not only not <u>envy</u>, but not <u>pitty</u> this <u>Monster</u>, do nothing? Yes, let him <u>laugh</u>. And if one of these <u>hot cholerick firebrands</u>, which nourish themselves by <u>quarrelling</u>, and kindling others, spit upon a <u>fool</u> one <u>sparke</u> of <u>disgrace</u>, he, like a <u>thatcht house</u> quickly burning, may be <u>angry</u>; but the <u>wise</u> man, as <u>cold</u> as the <u>Salamander</u>, may not only be <u>angry</u> with him, but not be <u>sorry</u> for him; therefore let him <u>laugh:</u> so he shall be known a Man, because he can <u>laugh</u>, a <u>wise Man</u> that he knows at <u>what</u> to <u>laugh</u>, and a <u>valiant Man</u> that he <u>dares</u> laugh: for he that <u>laughs</u> is justly reputed more <u>wise</u>, than at whom it is <u>laughed.</u>

And hence I think proceeds that which in
these later <u>formal</u> times I have much noted;
that now when our <u>superstitious</u> <u>civilitie</u> of
<u>manners</u> is become a mutuall <u>tickling</u>
<u>flattery</u> of one another, almost every man
affecteth an <u>humour</u> of <u>jesting</u>, and is
content to be <u>deject</u>, and to <u>deform</u> himself,
yea become <u>fool</u> to no other <u>end</u> that I
can spie, but to give his <u>wise Companion</u>
occasion to <u>laugh</u>; and to shew themselves
in <u>promptness</u> of <u>laughing</u> is so great in
<u>wise men</u>, that I think all <u>wise men</u>, if
any <u>wise men</u> do read this <u>Paradox</u>, will
<u>laugh</u> both at it and me.

Blessedness itself
is God himself;
our blessedness
is our possession;
our union with God.

In our Funerals, we ourselves have no
interest; there we cannot advise,
we cannot direct.

God vouchsafed to be made man for man.

Seek we then ourselvs in ourselvs; for
as Men force the Sun with much force to
pass by gathering his beams with a
crystal glass;

So we, If we into ourselves will turn,
Blowing our sparks of virtue, may outburn
The straw, which doth about our hearts
sojourne.

I do nothing
upon myself,
and yet am
mine own executioner.

Take heed of loving me.